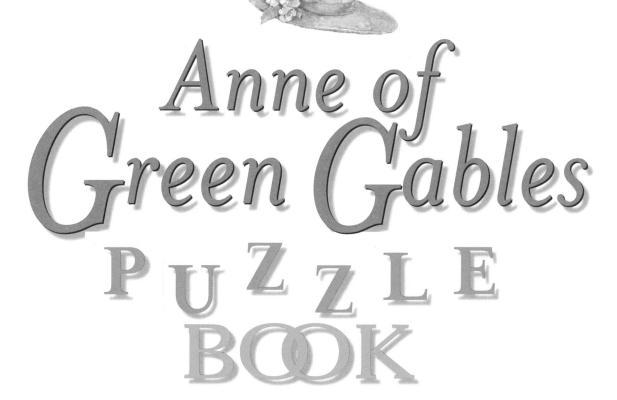

Anne of Green Gables
PUZZLE BOOK

BY MARION HOFFMANN
ILLUSTRATIONS BY MURIEL WOOD

Fitzhenry & Whiteside

Published in Canada by Fitzhenry & Whiteside, 195 Allstate Parkway, Markham, Ontario L3R 4T8

Published in the United States by Fitzhenry & Whiteside, 311 Washington Street, Brighton, Massachusetts 02135

www.fitzhenry.ca   godwit@fitzhenry.ca

10 9 8 7 6 5 4 3 2 1

Library and Archives Canada Cataloguing in Publication
Hoffmann, Marion, 1938-
Anne of Green Gables puzzle book / Marion Hoffmann ;
illustrated by Muriel Wood.
ISBN 978-1-55455-040-1 (pbk.)

1. Montgomery, L. M. (Lucy Maud), 1874-1942. Anne of Green Gables—Miscellanea.
2. Crossword puzzles. I. Wood, Muriel II. Title.
GV1507.C7H54 2007   jC813'.52   C2007-902286-3

U.S. Publisher Cataloging-in-Publication Data
(Library of Congress Standards)
Hoffmann, Marion.
Anne of Green Gables puzzle book / Marion Hoffmann ;
illustrated by Muriel Wood.
[64] p. : col. ill. ; cm.
Summary: A collection of crosswords and other word puzzles
based on L. M. Montgomery's Anne of Green Gables.

ISBN: 9781554550401 (pbk.)
1. Crossword puzzles – Juvenile literature.
2. Word games – Juvenile literature. I. Montgomery, L. M. (Lucy Maud), 1874-1942.
Anne of Green Gables. II. Title.
793.73 dc22 GV1507.H644 2007

Fitzhenry & Whiteside acknowledges with thanks the Canada Council for the Arts, and the Ontario Arts Council
for their support of our publishing program. We acknowledge the financial support of the Government of Canada
through the Book Publishing Industry Development Program (BPIDP) for our publishing activities.

Design by Tanya Montini

Printed in Canada

CONTENTS

Kindred Spirits

ACROSS

1 _____ Edward Island
3 Anne's new teacher
5 Rachel loved to give this
7 Marilla's brother
11 The Pye girl
12 Anne's bosom friend
13 Wine
14 Marilla's missing jewelry
15 Anne's gable
17 Marilla and Matthew _____
22 Green Gables village
24 Wrong cake ingredient
26 Story line
27 Anne's part in concert tableau
28 One of Matthew's favorite things
29 Matthew's horse
31 New reverend's wife, Mrs. _____
32 Anne loved this kind of spirit

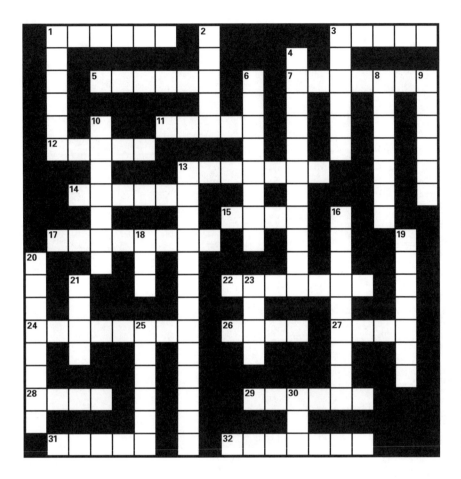

DOWN

1 Anne longed for these sleeves
2 Matthew's Christmas gift
3 What Anne's checkered dress was made of
4 Anne had a vivid one
6 Picnic treat (2 words)
8 Mother of twins, Mrs. _____
9 Tree in Diana's garden
10 What Gilbert called Anne
13 Island capital
16 Diana's aunt
18 What Marilla and Matthew ordered

19 The Blythe boy
20 Anne's first Avonlea teacher
21 Not Anne's color
23 Violet _____

25 Anne's age when she came to Green Gables
30 Color of P.E.I. roads

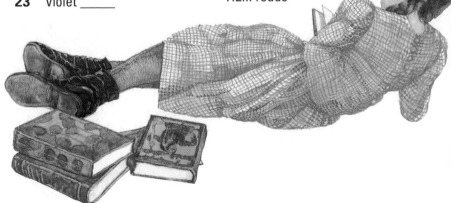

Naughty Anne

Anne often got into trouble. Afterwards she was always sorry, but she could never seem to help herself at the time. Decode these sentences to find out how Anne describes her troublesome habits.

In this code, A=1, B=2, C=3, and so on.

9 — 14 5 22 5 18 — 4 15 — 20 8 5 — 19 1 13 5
I **NEVER** **DO** **THE** **SAME**

14 1 21 7 8 20 25 — 20 8 9 14 7 — 20 23 9 3 5.
NAUGHTY **THING** **TWICE.**

20 8 1 20 ' 19 — 15 14 5 — 7 15 15 4 — 20 8 9 14 7
THAT'S **ONE** **GOOD** **THING**

1 2 15 21 20 — 13 5.
ABOUT **ME.**

Ghosts

Anne imagined all sorts of things.
"Oh, Marilla, I wouldn't go through the Haunted Wood
after dark now for anything. I'd be sure that white things
would reach out from behind the trees and grab me."

Here are the answers for the crossword. All you have to do is make them fit.

ANNE	GABLE	MATTHEW	QUEEN	SLATE
APPLES	GHOSTS	ORCHARD	RACHEL	WILLOW
AVONLEA	ISLAND	PASTURE	RED	WINE
DIANA	MARILLA			

The White Way of Delight

"When I don't like the name of a place or person I always imagine a new one," Anne told Matthew.

Match the names and words in column A with the statements in column B.

A

1. Cordelia
2. Gilbert Blythe
3. Raspberry cordial
4. The Haunted Wood
5. Minnie May
6. Queen's
7. Sorrel mare
8. Mrs. Spencer
9. Mrs. Hammond
10. Cavendish
11. Diana
12. The Avenue

B

a. She made "a bookmark out of red tissue paper."

b. The Cuthberts asked her to get them a boy.

c. Matthew jogged her "comfortably over the eight miles to Bright River."

d. The White Way of Delight

e. Mother of three sets of twins

f. Anne broke a slate over his head.

g. L. M. Montgomery lived here with her grandparents.

h. Anne's imaginary ghosts roamed there.

i. Anne gave Diana wine instead of this drink.

j. Matthew wanted Anne to go to this school.

k. Anne's imaginary name for herself

l. This little girl had croup.

The Haunted Wood

Nothing remained ordinary or "common place" for long when Anne's imagination went to work. For Anne and Diana, the spruce grove between Green Gables and the Barry's farm was transformed into the Haunted Wood.

"Oh, we have imagined the most harrowing things," Anne told Marilla. "There's a white lady walks along the brook just about this time of the night and wrings her hands and utters wailing cries … And there's a headless man stalks up and down the path and skeletons glower at you between the boughs."

```
C L D O O W D E T N U A H J T L R L E
D R Y A D S B U B B L E R D G Z C G M
F X X Z N K L M K F K G V K K N D W G
M L Y D N A L S I A I R O T C I V R J
W S P E N C E R V A L E R P R Z D Q C
O C X K X Q V R X V X B H B R N T E H
L X L Q N S T W G R C D W N O Y P M A
L P B R I G H T R I V E R P M O B G R
O F D V E S T I R J N R S N L R R Q L
H W V A N S W N T N Y Z S D E Z G O
S I I E A O D D W I R W D H E L T P T
E L O L L W P N N R N R O N M H H R T
D L L N S Q F C A A A G G T E X R R E
N O E O R U K B A H S A W A E J D R T
Y W T V E E C T C R B E V A X P N L O
L M V A E J R M L M E T L T K O C W
L E A N O N O W E Z N O B I Z E J H N
P R L R L P K S Q U L T D J H R R T N
T E E X K C B Y E N T N X Y M W L S Q
```

Find the words by looking horizontally, vertically, diagonally, backwards or forwards.

AVONLEA

BARRYS POND

BRIGHT RIVER

CARMODY

CHARLOTTETOWN

DRYADS BUBBLE

GREEN GABLES

HAUNTED WOOD

HOPETOWN

LOVERS LANE

LYNDES HOLLOW

NEWBRIDGE

ORCHARD SLOPE

SHINING WATERS

SNOW QUEEN

SPENCER VALE

THE AVENUE

VICTORIA ISLAND

VIOLET VALE

WHITE SANDS

WILLOWMERE

The Lily Maid

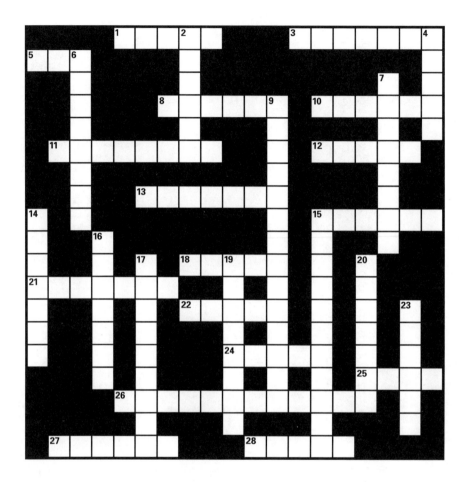

ACROSS

1 Anne liked stories with this
3 She said to Anne: "It's been fearsome lonely here without you."
5 Anne put blossoms in it
8 Rachel Lynde liked to make these
10 The lily maid
11 Avonlea club
12 Anne broke it when she fell
13 He was "such a sympathetic listener"
15 Matthew's favorite roses
18 Avonlea shopkeeper
21 Anne dreaded crossing these
22 Scholarship
24 Shape of candy Gilbert gave Anne
25 Hair keepsake
26 Anne loved writing these
27 _____ Bubble
28 It drowned in pudding sauce

DOWN

2 Anne longed for this hair color
4 Cuthberts' bank
6 It "cast a cloud" over Anne's whole life
7 One of Anne's imaginary friends
9 Minister stole one (2 words)
14 Anne's class rival
15 Anne learned this delicious word at the picnic
16 Anne bought hair dye from him
17 Aunt Josephine's house
19 Jewel in Marilla's brooch
20 How Anne and Diana communicated
23 Anne's ugly dress

Red Hair

"People who haven't red hair don't know what trouble is," Anne told Marilla. Decode this sentence to find out why Anne longed for black or auburn hair.

In this code, C=A, D=B, E=C; A=Y, B=Z, and so on.

```
T G F - J G C F G F     R G Q R N G
R E D - H E A D E D     P E O P L E

E C P ' V   Y G C T   R K P M,   P Q V   G X G P
C A N ' T   W E A R   P I N K,   N O T   E V E N

K P   K O C I K P C V K Q P.
I N   I M A G I N A T I O N.
```

Wild Cherry Tree

"It would be lovely to sleep in a wild cherry tree
all white with bloom in the moonshine,
don't you think?" Anne asked Matthew.

Here are the answers for the crossword. All you have to do is make them fit.

BIRCH	CHERRY	HOLLOW	OCEAN	ROMANTIC
BRIDGE	DIANA	JOSIAH	PLUM	SLATE
BROOCH	FRANK	KINDRED	PUFFED	SPRING
CARMODY	GULLS	LILAC	QUEENS	STELLA

Teachers

Anne's favorite teacher was Miss Stacy.
"I love Miss Stacy with my
whole heart," she told Marilla.

Match the names in column A with the quotations in column B.

A

1. Mrs. Allan

2. Gilbert

3. Miss Stacy

4. Mr. Phillips

5. Matthew

6. Josie Pye

7. Diana

8. Mr. Allan

9. Mrs. Lynde

10. Anne

11. Aunt Josephine

12. Marilla

B

a. "You seem to half believe your own imaginations."

b. "Well, they didn't pick you for your looks, that's sure and certain."

c. "She's such a little thing … Such an interesting little thing."

d. "Everybody should have a purpose in life and pursue it faithfully."

e. "Avonlea is a lovely name. It sounds just like music."

f. "I feel sick. I … I must go home."

g. "I'm afraid my imagination is a little rusty—it's so long since I used it."

h. "The time has come for us to part."

i. "I'll never ask you to be friends again, Anne Shirley."

j. "We couldn't be too careful what habits we formed and what ideals we aquired in our teens."

k. She said Anne "looked like a scarecrow."

l. She said that Anne was the "brightest and sweetest child she ever knew."

Trees and Flowers

At 14, Anne still had a vivid imagination that transformed ordinary places into enchanted landscapes. But there were no more headless horsemen and ghostly white ladies in the Haunted Wood.

"It's lovely in the woods now," an older Anne told Marilla. "All the little wood things—the ferns and the satin leaves and the crackerberries—have gone to sleep, just as if somebody had tucked them away until spring under a blanket of leaves. I think it was a little gray fairy with a rainbow scarf that came tiptoeing along the last moonlight night and did it."

```
P  S  F  M  T  L  R  L  M  L  I  L  A  C  S  P  S
H  T  D  O  A  N  C  V  O  F  S  M  J  E  J  P  Z
B  A  V  U  K  I  K  C  K  M  N  E  C  L  U  L  Z
C  R  M  N  T  S  S  Z  O  W  B  U  I  C  B  F  N
R  F  A  T  R  K  S  H  T  L  R  A  R  N  V  K  N
A  L  P  A  H  C  D  T  C  P  U  E  R  M  O  L  W
C  O  L  I  N  O  O  W  S  U  T  M  A  D  D  E  J
K  W  E  N  H  H  O  N  G  T  F  Y  B  A  I  D  P
E  E  N  A  X  Y  W  R  U  M  F  P  F  I  S  E  Y
R  R  K  S  R  L  H  B  K  L  T  F  B  L  N  S  S
B  S  H  H  M  L  C  K  O  C  O  V  L  N  R  E  K
E  N  N  R  P  O  E  W  G  D  W  E  M  T  H  S  S
R  S  R  I  F  H  E  H  I  K  B  D  Z  Q  D  O  G
R  F  N  G  H  R  B  L  Z  E  R  M  K  W  T  R  X
I  P  P  H  S  Q  S  R  N  Z  C  L  O  V  E  R  Q
E  T  N  I  M  K  W  U  N  H  T  E  A  R  O  S  E
S  Y  R  Q  H  Q  J  Z  S  U  S  S  I  C  R  A  N
```

Find the words by looking horizontally, vertically, diagonally,
backwards or forwards.

BEECHWOODS   HOLLYHOCKS   NARCISSUS

BUTTERCUPS   JUNEBELLS   PEONIES

CLOVER   LILACS   ROSES

COLUMBINES   LOMBARDIES   SPRUCE

CRACKERBERRIES   MAPLE   STARFLOWERS

DAFFODILS   MAYFLOWERS   TEA ROSE

FIRS   MINT

FUCHSIA   MOUNTAIN ASH

Eternal Farewell

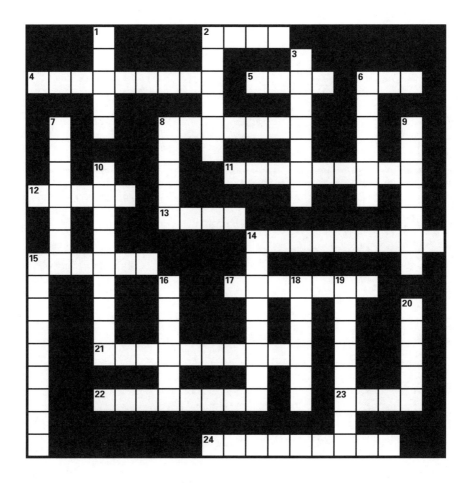

ACROSS

2 "What a splendid _____ he has," Anne says of Gilbert

4 Diana's aunt

5 What the school concert raised money for

6 Minutes to say "an eternal farewell"

8 Wine that got Diana drunk

11 Where Marilla found her brooch (2 words)

12 _____ afternoons: school activity

13 "Unromantic" meat

14 Kind of sewing Anne didn't like

15 Anne apologized to her

17 One of Diana's best features

21 Aunt Josephine took Anne and Diana to this event

22 Anne put apple _____ on the table

23 Anne thought it her best feature

24 Age Anne and Diana will put up their hair

DOWN

1 Anne dyed her hair this color

2 Preserves for tea

3 He loved to spoil Anne

6 Mr. Lynde

7 Anne wanted to call her aunt

8 Minnie May's illness

9 He saved Anne from drowning

10 Anne called it Idlewild

14 Anne's first Avonlea teacher

15 Josie Pye dared Anne to walk this

16 Anne wore her hair in them

18 Anne had a "scrumptious time" there

19 Exam before going to Queen's

20 _____ Maurice, Anne's imaginary friend

Depths of Despair

Anne was afraid Marilla and Matthew would send
her back to the orphanage. "I'm in the depths
of despair," she told them. Decode this sentence
to find out what else she said.

In this code, A=Z, B=Y, C=X, D=W, and so on.

G S R H   R H   G S V   N L H G
☐☐☐☐   ☐☐   ☐☐☐   ☐☐☐☐

G I Z T R X Z O   G S R M T   G S Z G
☐☐☐☐☐☐☐☐   ☐☐☐☐☐   ☐☐☐☐

V E V I   S Z K K V M V W   G L   N V.
☐☐☐☐   ☐☐☐☐☐☐☐☐☐   ☐☐   ☐☐.

Cordelia

Anne wanted a more unusual name, such as Cordelia. "It's such a perfectly elegant name," she told Marilla.

Here are the answers for the crossword. All you have to do is make them fit.

ALLAN   CLIFFS   GOSSAMER   MILTON   ROSE
BERRY   CLOVER   GROVES   PATH   SLOANE
BRAIDS   CORDELIA   LAURA   PEARL   VANILLA
BUBBLE   FRECKLES   LOGS   PEONIES   VIOLET

Poor Mouse

When a mouse drowned in Marilla's sauce, Anne said
she would "never forget that awful moment
if I live to be a hundred."

Match the names and words in column A with the statements in column B.

A

1. Goods

2. Aunt Josephine

3. Beau

4. Rosamond Montmorency

5. Mr. Bentley

6. Clever

7. Chatter

8. Jane Andrews

9. Rachel

10. Gilbert

11. Titian

12. Pudding

B

a. Anne used this nom de plume for her story-club tales.

b. She lent Anne an exciting new book.

c. Matthew thought that he "kind of liked Anne's _____."

d. A mouse drowned in the _____ sauce.

e. He recited "Bingen on the Rhine" at the concert.

f. "Why, she'll eat you alive," Diana told Anne.

g. An artist called Anne "the girl with the splendid _____ hair."

h. Anne asked Matthew: "Would you rather be divinely beautiful or dazzlingly _____ or angelically good?"

i. He was the minister before Mr. Allan.

j. She was surprised to see Matthew driving by wearing a white collar and his best suit.

k. Anne's carpetbag contained all her "worldly _____."

l. Gilbert's father was once Marilla's _____.

Anne's World

```
F G J K X L L K T D X S F T Y G R
N R M A R I L L A B Q W V H G N R
O E N M R N Z X P P C E W G E G M
S T Z F T N A L L A S R M I R H S
R L G H A I S O J R T D M R T M A
E U T E X L N M A W P N T W I A M
G O L B R V E I M L L A R E E T O
O B R L Q A L H M C G Y F I P T H
R M M V E E L I C I X L P Z Y H T
M A X A D B S D L A N L X Z E E D
F S D R R S A B I O R I K I Y W R
R L O G S Y E I E N N B M L D K B
T C H T E R A G L X E V V T Z Q Q
C N A D T X R L N U E L L A M A Y
Z C N F J U V H I H J M X K D R B
Y Y T M P Z J R Z C P V T F T L K
L F W S V Z V I O L E T T A T K J
```

Find the words by looking horizontally, vertically, diagonally, backwards or forwards.

BILLY ANDREWS	JULIA BELL	MRS ALLAN
CORDELIA	LIZZIE WRIGHT	RACHEL
ELLA MAY	LYNDE	ROGERSON
GERALDINE	MARILLA	SAM BOULTER
GERTIE PYE	MARY ALICE	SPURGEON
GILBERT	MATTHEW	THOMAS
JOSIAH	MISS STACY	VIOLETTA

Anne's Christmas

ACROSS

2 Where Matthew went to buy a dress

6 Anne longed to sleep in this kind of room

7 Anne's academic rival

10 Aunt Josephine's Christmas gift to Anne

11 _____ Sloane was "dead gone" on Anne

12 Rachel's Christmas gift to Anne

14 New friend at Queen's

17 What Diana did before she spoke

19 "Would you rather be divinely _____ or dazzlingly clever?"

21 One of Matthew's qualities

22 Gilbert pinned it to a chair

24 Anne secretly regretted she had not been born in _____

25 She said: "I believe in a girl being fitted to earn her own living."

DOWN

1 Aunt Josephine's niece

3 Miss _____ Stacy

4 Sunday school teacher, Miss _____

5 It held Anne's "worldly goods"

6 Avonlea doctor

8 Sharp-tongued girl

9 Matthew's first gift to Anne

12 She said: "Her temper matches her hair."

13 Money Anne used to buy hair dye

15 Anne's hat caused a stir there

16 Queen's Entrance _____

18 Concert recitation, *The _____ Vow*

19 Anne took one to the picnic

20 Gilbert's _____ was once Marilla's beau

21 What Matthew bought instead of a dress

22 Jane Andrews's brother

23 Anne wanted to be just like Mrs. _____

Gentle Matthew

Matthew Cuthbert was a shy, quiet man. But from the very beginning, he was on Anne's side. "Matthew Cuthbert," Marilla exclaimed, "I believe that child has bewitched you! I can see as plain as plain that you want to keep her."

"We might be some good to her," Matthew told Marilla. Decode this sentence to find out what else Matthew said about Anne.

In this code, A=2, B=3, C=4; Y=26, Z=27, and so on.

24 6 13 13   15 16 24,   20 9 6 ' 20
W E L L   N O W,   S H E ' S

2   19 6 2 13   15 10 4 6
A   R E A L   N I C E

13 10 21 21 13 6   21 9 10 15 8,   14 2 19 10 13 13 2.
L I T T L E   T H I N G,   M A R I L L A.

I'm Sorry, Mrs. Lynde

When Anne lost her temper with Rachel Lynde,
Marilla insisted that she apologize. Nobody could have
done it better. "I could never express all my sorrow, no,
not if I used up a whole dictionary," Anne told her.

Here are the answers for the crossword. All you have to do is make them fit.

APOLOGY	FLAG	JEWEL	REDMOND	STARS
BLOOM	FLORA	KATIE	SPARE	TASSEL
CHATTER	HARMON	MINNIE	SPIRIT	TEACHER
CONCH	HORIZON	PEDDLER	SPOIL	TRESSES

Minnie May and the Croup

When Minnie May was ill, Anne knew how to help her.
She had lots of experience. After all, she said,
"Mrs. Hammond had twins three times."

Match the names and words in column A with the statements in column B.

A

1. Ipecac

2. Excruciatingly

3. Tongue

4. Geometry

5. Apple

6. White collar

7. China

8. Miss Rogerson

9. Lace

10. William Bell

11. Buttercups

12. Feather tick

B

a. Sunday school teacher

b. Matthew wore one the day he met Anne at the station.

c. Anne wrestled with this when making her bed.

d. Anne put these flowers in her hat when she went to church.

e. Anne and Diana's playhouse was in his birch grove.

f. "Gilbert Blythe has hurt my feelings _____."

g. Marilla's good shawl was made of this.

h. Anne gave this medication to Minnie May.

i. After Anne saved Minnie May's life, Mrs. Barry served her tea on her best _____.

j. Gilbert's peace offering to Anne was a strawberry _____.

k. Anne said this was "casting a cloud over my whole life."

l. Marilla told Anne that her fall from the roof hadn't harmed this part of her body.

Colors

```
N R R K R B Q X Q E D P L J K T T
W W Q U T W L B U V M Q M T N R N
J X B W O E G L E D W W Z S I Y R
T Y Y L V O B V B K E B D Y P Z A
J W L U L E N O R A D B H E M V
M E A D K Q F G N T T K N T S J E
Y M E O K Q T R Y P H E K E O P N
N N M H W M W T B T E R N M R U B
E S N O R F F A S R R A T A D R L
M C N N E D A J G M G L R M L P A
I Y R B P T A E V G R D K L I L C
L M E I T V L I W D A Y N L W E K
T B V K M P N Q P H Y P C Z C C K
H Q L H P S G O B E I Z B R O W N
J G I A T R O X M V S T M R Q L D
R T S W O R A N G E Z V E Z L T T
T U R Q U O I S E L L N M B X B K
```

Find the words by looking horizontally, vertically, diagonally, backwards or forwards.

AMETHYST	LIME	SEPIA
APPLE GREEN	MAUVE	SILVER
BROWN	ORANGE	SMOKE BLUE
CRIMSON	PEARL	TURQUOISE
EBONY	PURPLE	WEATHER GRAY
GOLDEN	RAVEN BLACK	WHITE
JADE	RUBY	WILD ROSE PINK
LEMON	SAFFRON	YELLOW

The Amethyst Brooch

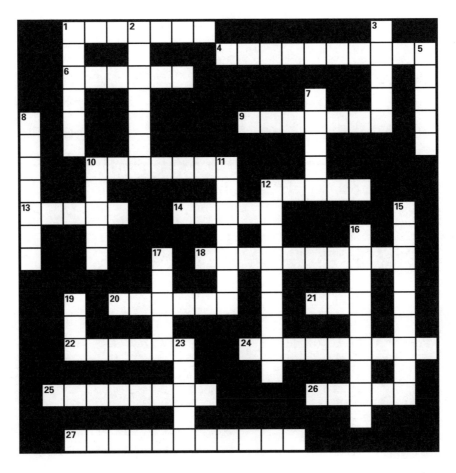

ACROSS

1 Avery scholarship college

4 Where Marilla thought she'd left her brooch

6 Tree outside Anne's window

9 She had eye problems

10 "I wouldn't give a dog I liked to that _____ woman."

12 A club

13 Anne walked the ridgepole for the sake of her _____

14 Diana took _____ lessons

18 Matthew gave Anne a string of them (2 words)

20 Lived in the Haunted Wood?

21 Currant wine was on this shelf

22 Popular Avonlea game

24 Gilbert won it at Queen's (2 words)

25 Mr. Allan's job

26 _____ Boute, Marilla's hired man

27 Ice cream defied it, said Anne

DOWN

1 _____ Lynde

2 She took care of the Barry children (2 words)

3 She got sick at Anne's tea party

5 Anne gave them to plants, trees, and water

7 _____ scarf, substitute for Elaine's gold cloth

8 "He had a spell with his heart."

10 Meeting place on way to school

11 Anne's cap was adorned with them

12 Josie Pye said Anne looked like one

15 She let her students think for themselves (2 words)

16 Avonlea girls loved these tarts

17 Color of dress Matthew gave Anne

19 Where Anne first met Aunt Josephine

23 Color of Anne's evening dress

Delights
of Anticipation

Anne dreamed about things long before they
happened—like the picnic and ice cream.
"I guess ice cream is one of those things that
are beyond imagination," she told Marilla.
Decode the sentence to find out why Anne
spent so much time anticipating things.

In this code, A=3, B=4, C=5; Y=27, Z=28, and so on.

14 17 17 13 11 16 9   8 17 20 25 3 20 6   22 17

22 10 11 16 9 21   11 21   10 3 14 8   22 10 7

18 14 7 3 21 23 20 7   17 8   22 10 7 15.

Horrid Josie Pye

Josie Pye was always mean to Anne, but she was especially horrid when she challenged Anne to do something dangerous: "I dare you to climb up there and walk the ridgepole of Mr. Barry's kitchen roof."

Here are the answers for the crossword. All you have to do is make them fit.

ANKLE	CONCERT	FAREWELL	RAVEN	STACY
AVERY	DEEP	FUN	ROOF	TART
BARRY	DORY	JOSIE	ROSS	WOODLAND
BOUGHS	DRUNK	POEM	RUSTY	
CHILD	FAIRY	PYE	SHADOW	

Liniment Cake

When the new minister and his wife are invited to tea at Green Gables, Anne's excitement boils over. "Will you let me make a cake for the occasion?" she asks Marilla. "I'd love to do something for Mrs. Allan, and you know I can make a pretty good cake by this time."

Match the names and words in column A with the statements in column B.

A

1. Aunt Josephine

2. Gilbert

3. Sacrifice

4. Abbey Bank

5. Mrs. Spencer

6. Charity

7. Marilla

8. Butter

9. Anodyne

10. Rachel Lynde

11. Murders

12. Matthew

B

a. Anne took part in a tableau called "Faith, Hope, and _____."

b. Anne accidentally put this liniment in her cake.

c. Anne called her "a most hospitable lady."

d. Anne thought Diana put too many of these in her stories.

e. Marilla said he always took Anne's part.

f. Rachel won an Exhibition prize for this.

g. She said: "Mark my words, Marilla Cuthbert'll live to rue the step she took."

h. Anne said: "I don't think I should let Gilbert make such a _____ for me."

i. He tied with Anne on the Entrance exam.

j. She said to Anne: "You've been my joy and comfort ever since you came to Green Gables!"

k. Mathew died when he learned of its failure.

l. Matthew said: "There never was a luckier mistake than what _____ made."

The Picnic

When Anne returns home from the Sunday School picnic, she can't contain her excitement—or hold her tongue. "Mr. Harmon Andrews took us all for a row on the Lake of Shining Waters ... And Jane Andrews nearly fell overboard ... I wish it had been me. It would have been such a romantic experience to have been nearly drowned ... And we had the ice cream. Words fail me to describe that ice cream. Marilla, I assure you it was sublime."

```
H A T E F U L D H L L D J G N L R
M W O N D E R F U L N H S I G R M
C K R B L Y T L B E B N K R N K X
K O Y P R A O Y I C C O I R I N L
I N N T L Y C R K C G I N E K G S
M M E S A P F I D L L T N S O N K
F O A L O M I I G P L I Y I O L U
P V T G O L M H N A C B N S L C N
M Y N S I P A D S W M M C T D R K
L T O V L N Y T J D M A I I O I C
F B T E Q P A Q I Z N H N B O N A
Z M S N P K G T B O T E C L G K B
R O M A N T I C I H N X I E P L B
N T H J M Q X W G O C N P R N Y A
S E L K C E R F W N N K N Q F C G
T R A G I C A L C B R I D E S L E
G T I R I P S D E R D N I K Y L N
```

Find the words by looking horizontally, vertically, diagonally, backwards or forwards.

AMBITION	GOOD LOOKING	PICNIC
BOSOM FRIEND	HAPPY	POETRY
BRIDES	HATEFUL	ROMANTIC
CONSOLATION	IMAGINATION	SKINNY
CRINKLY	IRRESISTIBLE	SKUNK CABBAGE
DIMPLES	KINDRED SPIRIT	TRAGICAL
FRECKLES	LOYALTY	WONDERFUL
FRIENDSHIP	MAGICAL	

Lady Fitzgerald

ACROSS

1 Matthew tells Anne not to give up all her _____

4 Anne loved to day_____

6 Anne and Diana were bosom _____

7 Ruby played King _____

9 Where Matthew went for Anne (2 words)

12 Diana's hair color

13 Lady _____ Fitzgerald

14 Marilla taught Anne to say these

15 Anne's school after Avonlea

19 They were on Anne's evening dress

20 Anne: "I will always love thee, _____."

22 Why Anne was made to sit beside Gilbert

26 Mr. and Mrs. Chester _____

27 Moody _____ MacPherson

28 Gilbert put this in his breast pocket at the concert

DOWN

2 Anne put her clothes on it

3 Diana: "_____ is aw'fly handsome, Anne."

5 Name in P.E.I.

8 Anne often felt _____ with Mrs. Lynde

10 Anne and Gilbert studied to become _____

11 Prettiest girl at Queen's (2 words)

12 Mr. _____, Diana's father

16 Marilla stopped this to save her eyes

17 _____ Sands Hotel

18 Dying her hair cured Anne of this

19 They dotted Anne's face

21 Minnie May was Diana's _____

22 Anne's teacher fancied _____ Andrews

23 Anne's favorite animals at the Exhibition

24 Anne's birthday month

25 Anne's sensible friend

As Glad
As Glad Can Be

When Marilla told Anne that she was staying at Green Gables, Anne proclaimed she was "as glad as glad can be." And then she asked, "Can I call you Aunt Marilla?" Decode this sentence to find another question Anne asked Marilla that day.

In this code, A=C, B=D, C=E; Y=A, Z=B, and so on.

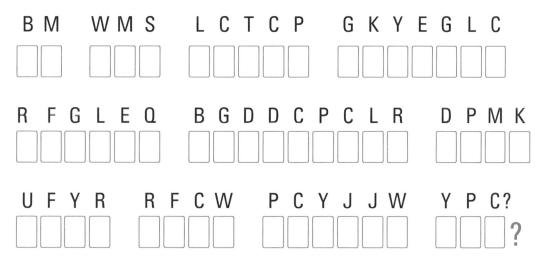

B M   W M S   L C T C P   G K Y E G L C

☐☐   ☐☐☐   ☐☐☐☐☐   ☐☐☐☐☐☐☐

R F G L E Q   B G D D C P C L R   D P M K

☐☐☐☐☐☐   ☐☐☐☐☐☐☐☐☐   ☐☐☐☐

U F Y R   R F C W   P C Y J J W   Y P C?

☐☐☐☐   ☐☐☐☐   ☐☐☐☐☐☐   ☐☐☐?

The Wincey Dress

When Anne arrived at Green Gables, she was wearing "this horrid old wincey dress." So she just imagined that she "had on the most beautiful pale blue silk dress" instead.

Here are the answers for the crossword. All you have to do is make them fit.

ACADEMY   FRIEND   MAPLE   ROCKER   SLEIGH
CHIMES   GATE   MOONLIGHT   SHIRLEY   SPRUCE
EMMA   LOVE   MUSK   SILVER   TREES
FIELD   LYNDE   PIGEON   SLEEVES   WINCEY

Puffed Sleeves

Anne longed for a pretty dress with puffed sleeves.
It arrived on Christmas Day—a gift from Matthew.
"Matthew, it's perfectly exquisite," Anne exclaimed.

Match the names and words in column A with the statements in column B.

A

1. Matthew

2. Rosebud

3. White

4. Rival

5. Dreams

6. Waters

7. Dictionary

8. Puffed sleeves

9. Teacher's

10. Affliction

11. Scope

12. Garden rake

B

a. Anne called one of her stories *The Jealous* _____.

b. Matthew's unnecessary purchase

c. Anne believed she was the only girl in Avonlea without them.

d. He said: "I guess my putting in my oar occasional never did much harm after all."

e. Anne went to Queen's to get a First Class _____ License.

f. Anne said it was easier to "bear up under _____ on a sunshiny day."

g. What Anne needed for her imagination.

h. Anne's "highest idea of earthly bliss" was to have a _____ dress.

i. In their first hour together, Anne asked Matthew: "_____ don't often come true, do they?"

j. Lake of Shining _____

k. Anne said to Mrs. Lynde: "I could never express all my sorrow, no, not if I used up a whole _____."

l. Marilla saved this tea set for special visitors.

Bouncing Bets

Anne first met Diana in Mrs. Barry's beautiful garden. "There were rosy bleeding-hearts and great splendid crimson peonies; white, fragrant narcissi and thorny sweet Scotch roses; pink and blue and white columbines and lilac-tinted Bouncing Bets ... a garden it was where sunshine lingered and bees hummed, and wind, beguiled into loitering, purred and rustled."

```
K  Z  L  P  I  G  E  O  N  B  E  R  R  I  E  S  C
S  T  F  S  R  E  W  O  L  F  K  S  U  M  L  H  R
E  C  W  R  B  S  U  C  O  R  C  F  A  Q  E  B  D
I  L  B  E  B  M  S  L  W  H  M  I  T  S  V  O  K
L  C  W  E  L  O  Z  A  C  A  S  O  T  T  O  N  M
I  H  K  R  W  P  U  R  R  H  T  N  S  W  L  K  O
L  E  Q  T  I  D  I  N  C  G  U  E  N  S  F  C  U
E  R  R  E  L  B  K  U  C  T  N  R  R  L  F  W  N
C  R  Y  L  D  C  F  N  Z  I  E  O  P  F  Q  K  T
I  Y  R  P  P  M  T  Z  O  H  N  E  B  C  E  F  A
R  T  I  P  L  Z  C  Q  T  I  O  G  G  B  Z  R  I
L  R  F  A  U  K  W  U  B  N  L  J  B  L  I  X  N
Y  E  F  G  M  P  O  N  I  T  D  E  L  E  Y  R  A
X  E  Y  J  R  S  R  E  N  P  H  L  D  V  T  R  S
L  T  E  A  R  O  S  E  T  Y  G  R  W  N  L  S  H
R  N  L  H  O  N  E  Y  S  U  C  K  L  E  A  W  Q
P  B  L  E  E  D  I  N  G  H  E  A  R  T  M  D  M
```

Find the words by looking horizontally, vertically, diagonally,
backwards or forwards.

APPLE TREE	FIR	RIBBON GRASS
BIRCH	FUCHSIA	RICE LILIES
BLEEDING HEART	HONEYSUCKLE	SOUTHERNWOOD
BOUNCING BETS	MOSS	TEA ROSE
CHERRY TREE	MOUNTAIN ASH	WATER FERN
CHESTNUT	MUSK FLOWERS	WILD PLUM
CROCUS	PEONIES	
DANDELION	PIGEON BERRIES	

Diana

ACROSS

1   Where the ridgepole ran
3   He visited cousins in New Brunswick
9   _____ Alice Bell
11 Artist called Anne's hair this color
12 Diana lived at _____ Slope
14 Anne's school
16 Mrs. _____ would take Anne off the Cuthberts' hands
17 Fashionable sleeves
19 Mrs. _____ called Anne "desperately wicked"
21 Violet _____
23 What Anne did her first night at Green Gables
24 Mrs. _____ Spencer
27 She lived in Charlottetown
28 Anne had tea with Mrs. Allan there

DOWN

1   _____ Gillis
2   Anne and Diana had their _____ told for ten cents
4   It contained a braid of hair
5   She "has got mellow," Rachel said
6   He called Anne "a real nice little thing"
7   P.E.I. is on the Gulf of St. _____
8   Queen's city
10 Anne said she never made the same _____ twice
13 It was in William Bell's birch grove
14 Anne renamed it the White Way of Delight
15 Disappointment plunged Anne into "deeps of _____"
16 Diana was Anne's _____ friend
18 Anne looked after them better than she washed dishes
20 A new Queen's friend
22 Where Marilla often had pain
25 Anne said she had "a perfectly lovely name"
26 Anne longed to have hair that was _____ black

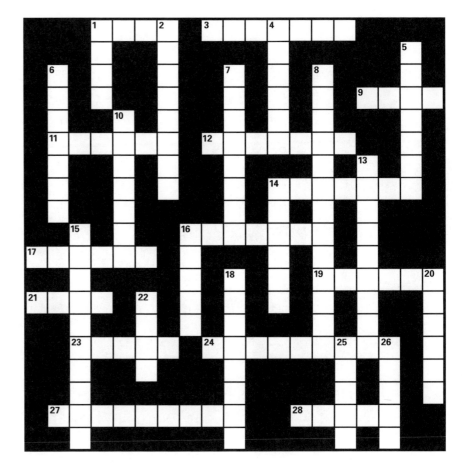

Prince Edward Island

"I've always heard that Prince Edward Island was
the prettiest place in the world, and I used to imagine
I was living here, but I never really expected I would.
It's delightful when your imaginations come true, isn't it?"
Decode the following sentences to find out what else
Anne said to Matthew about Prince Edward Island.

In this code, C=A, D=B, E=C; A=Y, B=Z, and so on.

V J K U   K U N C P F   K U   V J G

[THIS] [ISLAND] [IS] [THE]

D N Q Q O K G U V   R N C E G.   K   L W U V

[BLOOMIEST] [PLACE]. [I] [JUST]

N Q X G   K V   C N T G C F A.

[LOVE] [IT] [ALREADY].

page 39

The East Gable

On her first morning with the Cuthberts, Anne looked out the window of her room and fell in love with Green Gables. "Wasn't it a lovely place?" she thought. "Suppose she wasn't really going to stay here! She would imagine she was. There was scope for imagination here."

Here are the answers for the crossword. All you have to do is make them fit.

ANDREWS	CROUP	LAURA	PROVERB	SISTER
BOOK	DRYADS	LOYALTY	ROOM	WATERS
CAKE	EAST	MAY	RUBY	WINE
CANDLE	FUCHSIA	MURIEL	SCHOOL	
CHESTNUT	HONEY	MYRTLE	SHELF	

Gilbert

"Gilbert reached across the aisle, picked up the end of Anne's long red braid, held it out at arm's length and said in a piercing whisper: 'Carrots! Carrots!'"

Match the names in column A with the statements in column B.

A

1. Aunt Josephine

2. Jane Andrews

3. Mr. Phillips

4. Miss Stacy

5. Ruby Gillis

6. Rachel Lynde

7. Gilbert

8. Mrs. Allan

9. Jerry Boute

10. Mrs. Barry

11. Anne

12. Diana

B

a. "I've grown so interested in my pupils here that I found I couldn't leave them."

b. "I must do it. My honor is at stake."

c. "Gilbert Blythe teases the girls something terrible."

d. "I'm awfully sorry I made fun of your hair, Anne."

e. "I don't envy you bringing *that* up, Marilla."

f. "I don't think you are a fit little girl for Diana to associate with."

g. Marilla employs him to help around the farm.

h. She told Anne she had once been "a dunce at geometry."

i. She meant to have a beau as soon as she was fifteen.

j. "So, you've come to see me at last, you Anne-girl."

k. She thought "puffed sleeves were too worldly for a minister's wife."

l. "Take those flowers out of your hair and sit with Gilbert Blythe."

Dryad's Bubble

The day that Anne meets Diana, the girls become bosom friends and begin spinning plans for all the things they will do together. "We're going to the shore some day to gather shells," Anne tells Marilla. "We have agreed to call the spring down by the log bridge the Dryad's Bubble. Isn't that a perfectly elegant name? I read a story once about a spring called that. A dryad is sort of a grown-up fairy, I think."

```
D  N  N  X  I  M  A  G  I  N  A  T  I  O  N  D  F
R  R  W  S  L  L  E  B  H  G  I  E  L  S  M  S  D
M  Q  Y  P  I  H  S  D  N  E  I  R  F  R  R  R  R
D  O  T  A  Q  K  K  R  E  H  C  G  Z  A  X  H  Z
E  D  O  N  D  Y  Y  N  G  E  R  U  T  S  A  P  V
T  L  L  N  E  Q  P  M  D  E  J  S  H  A  D  O  W
N  A  B  S  L  M  T  P  I  Y  L  N  J  F  K  B  N
E  U  G  C  F  I  G  B  R  N  O  B  I  R  L  R  K
C  G  K  H  I  Y  G  R  B  Z  L  R  A  L  L  A  L
S  H  R  O  N  Y  P  H  I  T  E  N  E  G  M  I  N
W  T  H  L  C  P  L  R  T  F  K  H  M  H  A  N  O
T  E  P  A  H  W  O  L  L  T  S  Z  O  N  H  B  T
B  R  A  R  I  H  I  I  E  H  C  C  L  H  G  O  E
K  Q  R  S  M  H  E  N  C  J  E  R  N  T  N  W  L
K  R  E  H  E  S  T  N  C  A  D  K  R  B  I  L  E
G  K  S  I  S  W  O  Q  N  E  F  E  F  X  G  V  K
D  Z  L  P  T  C  F  P  X  Z  Y  D  R  E  A  M  S
```

Find the words by looking horizontally, vertically, diagonally,
backwards or forwards.

BRIDGE	HORIZON	SCHOLARSHIP
CONCH SHELL	IMAGINATION	SERAPH
DREAMS	LAUGHTER	SHADOW
DRYAD	MOONLIGHT	SKELETON
ELFIN CHIMES	OCEAN	SLEIGH BELLS
FIREFLIES	PASTURE	STARS
FRIENDSHIP	RAINBOW	WINCEY
GABLE	RED JELLY	
GINGHAM	SCENTED	

Hateful Boy!

ACROSS

2 What Anne's new cap was made of

8 Anne was "twitted about it"

9 Number of sets of Hammond twins

10 Color of Anne's new coat

12 Red hair was Anne's "lifelong _____"

14 Marilla had a sense of _____

17 Anne longed to sing in the Sunday School _____

21 She took Diana and Anne to the Exhibition

24 It cured Minnie May's croup

25 Puffed _____

28 Anne was afraid to walk there after dark (2 words)

30 She made Anne confess

31 _____ Sloane

DOWN

1 He thought Anne was "as smart as they make them"

3 Lady Cordelia wore a dress of "trailing white _____"

4 He wrote the lily maid poem

5 The "mean hateful boy"

6 Anne apologized to Mrs. Lynde on her _____

7 When Anne confessed, Aunt Josephine _____

11 Anne's mother's name

13 Anne called herself a "little _____ girl"

15 Anne said they had "besetting sins, just like everybody else"

16 Lake of _____ Waters

18 L.M. Montgomery lived there

19 Mr. Phillips was always curling it

20 He often said, "Well, I dunno."

22 Nom de _____

23 Ruby Gillis wanted many when she grew up

26 _____ May Spurgeon

27 Anne's best feature

29 Gilbert rescued Anne in one

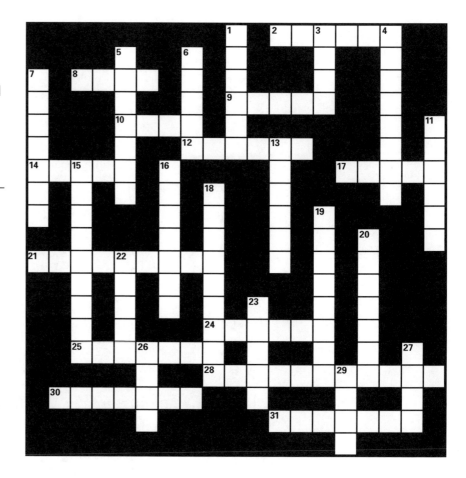

Dreadful Thin

On their way to Green Gables, Anne sized herself up for Matthew. "I AM dreadful thin, ain't I? There isn't a pick on my bones." Decode this sentence to find out what Anne longed for.

In this code, A=Z, B=Y, C=X, D=W, and so on.

R WL OLEV GL
I DO LOVE TO

RNZTRMV R SZEV
IMAGINE I HAVE

WRNKOVH RM NB VOYLDH.
DIMPLES IN MY ELBOWS.

The Evening Dress

Before Anne left for Queen's, Marilla surprised her with a new evening gown—a green dress "made up with many tucks and frills and shirrings."

Here are the answers for the crossword. All you have to do is make them fit.

APPLE	DREAMS	RACHEL	SLED	TEMPER
BRAIDS	FRILLS	ROSES	STAR	TROUBLE
BRIDGE	HOPES	RUBY	SUGAR	TUCKS
CHERRY	JERRY	SCHOLARSHIP		
DIANA	LYNDE	SLATE		

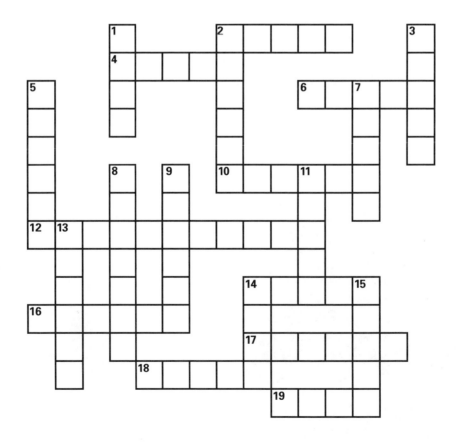

Off to Queen's

Marilla asked Anne if she wanted to go to Queen's
in Charlottetown and study for her teacher's license.
"It's been the dream of my life," Anne told her,
"—at least for the last six months."

Match the names and words in column A with the statements in column B.

A

1. Feet

2. Avery

3. Slippers

4. Josie Pye

5. Academy

6. Brooch

7. Rachel Lynde

8. Maid

9. Katie Maurice

10. Mrs. Blewett

11. Wife

12. Miss Stacy

B

a. She said: "Town's too jolly after that poky old Avonlea."

b. She would be "a terrible worker and driver."

c. She was "a red-hot politician."

d. "Her sleeve puffs are bigger than anybody else's in Avonlea."

e. She "lived" in Mrs. Thomas's bookcase.

f. Anne was a _____ of honor in *The Fairy Queen*.

g. According to Anne, fairies wore them on their feet.

h. "It's always wrong to do anything you can't tell
the minister's _____."

i. Anne went to the _____ at Queen's.

j. Anne's scholarship at Queen's

k. Marilla's most treasured possession

l. Anne "ground Gilbert's candy beneath her _____."

Ruby Gillis

```
F N L A U R A S P E N C E R V K C N M
Z C H E S T E R R O S S N B E N Z C T
C R T T S X Y L D J L T K R C E J M P
N E S Y D W T A T I C K E H C L K I E
O V I Q E F E X L N A V N I R M C N N
S O L T T R T R D C E N R Q Y X D N A
P L L J H L E N D D L U A R J R P I O
M G I T E B T T M N A R T B A M F E L
A Y G R L H M A L M A L A N A Z C M S
S M Y A M J R A E U E N Y E M R V A A
A M B C A T J I M B O A O E P B R Y I
H I U H R D T L E I B M M D M H Y H
T J R E R A Z L L A E M E R R W F R P
R L B L K K L B L M A W H I V A C C O
E X C L J T Y L L W T T I L L R H K S
B G V Y H H E R H N M D B L G L J C Q
T T B N Y T R I V H Y G C F S Z I N D
L L L D S P T D Z W N K L X Z O Z T W
P W X E V E R E N A J A R O L F N N M
```

Find the names by looking horizontally, vertically, diagonally, backwards or forwards.

BERTHA SAMPSON	HARMON ANDREWS	PEARL CLAY
BERTRAM DEVERE	JIMMY GLOVER	RACHEL LYNDE
CHESTER ROSS	KATIE MAURICE	RUBY GILLIS
DIANA BARRY	LAURA SPENCER	SOPHIA SLOANE
EMMA WHITE	MAMIE WILSON	STELLA MAYNARD
ETHEL MARR	MINNIE MAY	TILLIE BOULTER
FLORA JANE	MYRTLE BELL	

Currant Wine

ACROSS

1   Anne liked to use long ones
3   Anne thought white birches looked like these
8   P.E.I. is in this country
9   Raspberry _____
11   Miss Rogerson taught at this school
13   Mr. Allan's job
14   Popular Avonlea game
16   Anne wore a sailor _____
19   Geometry was Anne's _____ block
23   Flavoring Anne should have put in the cake
24   Anne wished she could call Marilla this
25   Aunt Josephine's was a little rusty
26   Rachel had this illness
28   Anne's bedding was a _____ tick

DOWN

1   What Anne called Mr. Barry's pond
2   Matthew loved to _____ Anne
4   Miss _____ tutored the Queen's students
5   Mr. Phillips said Anne's was disgraceful
6   She thought it likely Anne's parents "were nice folks"
7   What Anne did after her fall
10   _____ Andrews
11   Word on Gilbert's candy
12   She had black hair and rosy cheeks
14   Currant wine made Diana _____
15   _____ Gillis

17   A dress was Matthew's _____ gift
18   What Anne thought of boiled pork
19   Anne was afraid of seeing one in the Haunted Wood
20   Anne and Diana made them out of roseberries
21   Marilla and Rachel liked doing this
22   Marilla served Chester Ross plum _____
27   "Those _____ girls are cheats all round."

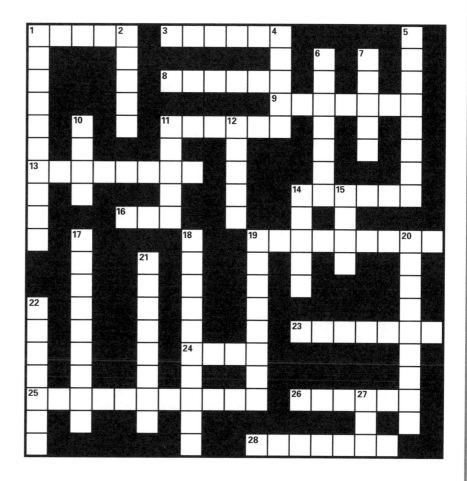

So Many Questions

Anne was always asking questions. "Isn't it splendid to think of all the things there are to find out about?" she asked Matthew. Decode the sentence to find out why Anne asked so many questions.

In this code, 1=Z, 2=Y, 3=X, and so on.

19 12 4 — HOW
26 9 22 — ARE
2 12 6 — YOU
20 12 18 13 20 — GOING

7 12 — TO
21 18 13 23 — FIND
12 6 7 — OUT
26 25 12 6 7 — ABOUT

7 19 18 13 20 8 — THINGS
18 21 — IF
2 12 6 — YOU
23 12 13 ' 7 — DON'T

26 8 16 — ASK
10 6 22 8 7 18 12 13 8 ? — QUESTIONS?

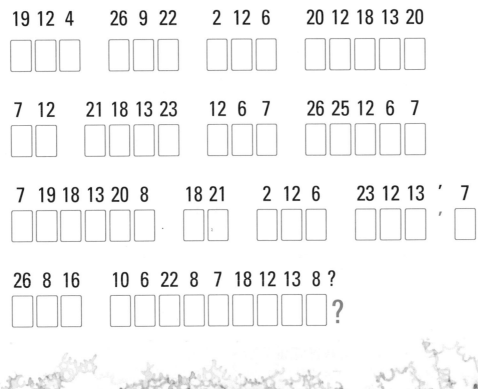

School Days

"The little girls of Avonlea school always pooled their lunches, and to eat three raspberry tarts all alone or even to share them only with one's best chum would have forever and ever branded as 'awful mean' the girl who did it. And yet, when the tarts were divided among ten girls, you just got enough to tantalize you."

Here are the answers for the crossword. All you have to do is make them fit.

AVERY   GILBERT   MEDAL   PINK   SCHOOL
BOAT   GREEK   MURIEL   POND   STACY
CROCUS   LATIN   MUSIC   REDMOND   TART
EDUCATION MAPLE   PHILLIPS   RUBY   TEACHER

Big Words

"People laugh at me because I use big words," Anne told Matthew. "But if you have big ideas you have to use big words to express them, haven't you?"

Match the missing words in column A with the quotations from Anne in column B.

A

1. Trial

2. Cry

3. Ice cream

4. Hopes

5. Hair

6. Failing

7. Tomorrow

8. Dream

9. Loving

10. Imagine

11. Despair

12. Delicious

B

a. "Marilla, isn't it nice that _____ is a new day with no mistakes in it yet?"

b. "I'm afraid I'm going to be a dreadful _____ to you, Marilla."

c. "When you are imagining something, you might as well _____ something worthwhile."

d. "It's so hard to keep from _____ things, isn't it?"

e. "I had one chocolate caramel once two years ago, and it was simply _____."

f. "I love a book that makes me _____."

g. "Next to trying and winning, the best thing is trying and _____."

h. "Can you eat when you are in the depths of _____?"

i. "Well, that is another hope gone. My life is a perfect graveyard of buried _____."

j. "I guess _____ is one of those things that defies imagination."

k. "Do you know, one can _____ so much better in a room where there are pretty things."

l. "Diana gave me a lock of her _____, and I'm going to sew it up in a little bag and wear it around my neck all my life."

Doctor Spencer

```
R  W  F  R  L  W  O  L  L  O  W  S  E  D  N  Y  L  N  K
K  M  M  D  E  M  U  R  I  E  L  S  T  A  C  Y  O  L  T
T  T  Y  Q  Y  C  N  V  C  L  O  V  E  R  C  S  O  X  Q
X  K  E  N  M  T  N  E  L  P  M  I  D  W  E  V  N  F  K
S  T  O  E  E  N  D  E  N  W  J  R  C  Y  E  R  Q  N  F
D  Z  J  W  D  R  R  N  P  M  H  S  N  R  J  B  T  K  V
N  V  Y  B  A  M  G  C  K  S  N  M  S  G  K  X  R  T  S
A  R  R  R  C  S  U  C  O  I  R  L  X  K  T  A  N  E  F
S  T  A  I  A  E  N  S  W  P  A  O  C  K  L  U  L  P  C
E  J  M  D  K  L  F  T  L  N  P  U  T  C  A  B  W  R  R
T  O  G  G  M  K  F  N  E  I  R  I  N  C  A  P  E  E  O
I  S  N  E  J  C  W  K  A  R  N  O  C  G  O  Z  H  N  U
H  E  U  Q  K  E  L  M  A  L  T  I  N  E  M  D  T  O  P
W  P  O  T  K  R  L  N  T  L  L  E  P  N  F  R  T  T  M
Q  H  Y  B  F  F  T  P  I  P  E  I  Z  E  T  R  A  S  H
C  I  T  H  B  W  F  M  L  R  X  R  R  R  C  R  M  D  W
L  N  H  G  I  M  Q  B  G  M  W  B  R  A  M  A  D  N  N
K  E  G  N  I  T  L  I  U  Q  L  H  X  O  M  K  C  A  Y
V  M  E  H  J  X  M  M  G  R  O  V  E  K  S  P  Y  S  G
```

Find the words by looking horizontally, vertically, diagonally, backwards or forwards.

ACADEMY	GREEN GABLES	MUSLIN
AUNT	GROVE	NEWBRIDGE
CLOVER	IPECAC	NOSE
COPPICE	JOSEPHINE	QUILTING
CROUP	LOVERS LANE	SANDSTONE
CURRANT WINE	LYNDES HOLLOW	SORREL
DIMPLE	MARILLA	TWINS
DOCTOR SPENCER	MATTHEW	WHITE SANDS
FRECKLES	MURIEL STACY	YOUNG MARY JOE

Play-Acting

ACROSS

3 Anne's romantic fictional hero
5 She said: "Handsome is as handsome does."
6 Anne wasn't born for _____ life
8 Marilla's friend
9 Mrs. _____ called play-acting "wicked"
10 Matthew's age when Anne arrived
14 Anne and Diana said an "eternal _____"
15 Tree outside Anne's window
17 Marilla: "We're not in the habit of shutting people in dark damp _____."
18 Number of glasses of currant wine Diana drank
19 Anne's birthplace
23 Avonlea teacher
24 _____ Queen
25 Queen in the lily maid poem
26 Diana was always "poring over a _____"
27 Matthew's Christmas gift
28 Anne's future career

DOWN

1 Sweet-smelling Island shrub
2 Anne broke it over Gilbert's head
3 Diana's surname
4 They bloom pink and white in spring
6 Debating _____
7 _____ spirit
8 These are hard to carry out when "irresistible temptations come"

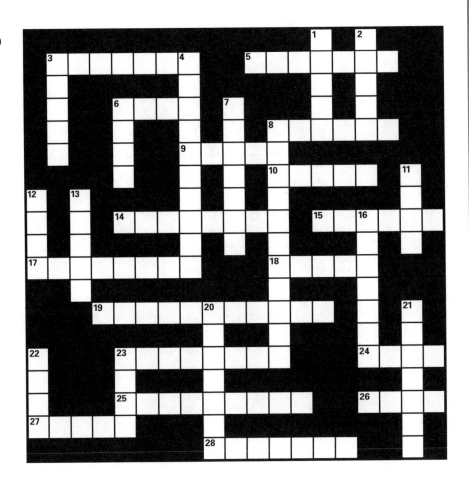

11 "You might as well tell Matthew not to breathe as not to _____."
12 M in L.M. Montgomery
13 Who said, "I love you devotedly, Anne"?
16 Anne and Gilbert decided not to be _____
20 Anne refused to say this name
21 Anne had to make one to Mrs. Lynde
22 What Diana loved to do
23 Anne wanted to give "drowned mouse" sauce to them

Books

Anne loved to read, but sometimes she had to resort to drastic measures until her homework was done. "I think I'll carry that book into the sitting room and lock it in the jam closet and give you the key. And you must NOT give it to me, Matthew, until my lessons are done, not even if I implore you on my bended knees." Decode this sentence to find out what Anne liked to read most.

In this code, 1=A, 2=B, 3=C, 4=D, and so on.

9   12 15 22 5   1   2 15 15 11

□   □□□□   □   □□□□

20 8 1 20   13 1 11 5 19   13 5   3 18 25.

□□□□   □□□□□   □□   □□□.

A Crushed Heart

After calling her "Carrots," Gilbert gave Anne
a small pink candy heart. Anne dropped it
to the floor and crushed it with
the heel of her shoe.

Here are the answers for the crossword. All you have to do is make them fit.

ANNE
BERRIES
BLOSSOM
CANDY
CARROTS

CUTHBERT
GARLAND
GATE
GHOST
IPECAC

ISLAND
LANE
LOVE
NOSE

PEARL
PRISSY
PYE
ROOF

SIXTY
SORREL
TANTRUM

Friends and Families

At the end of her studies at Queen's, Anne finally
went home to Green Gables, back to Marilla and Matthew,
back to Diana, Rachel, and Mrs. Allan, back to all the friends
and families who had watched her grow up in Avonlea.

Match the names in column A with the names in column B.

A	B
1. Pye	a. Lynde
2. Priscilla	b. Spurgeon
3. Moody	c. Marilla
4. Jerry	d. Diana
5. Chester	e. Gilbert
6. Cuthbert	f. Anne
7. Jane	g. Ruby
8. Barry	h. Grant
9. Shirley	i. Andrews
10. Rachel	j. Josie
11. Blythe	k. Ross
12. Gillis	l. Boute

The Lake of Shining Waters

The Lake of Shining Waters was a special place for Anne during her growing-up days at Green Gables. It represented all that was good in her life.

Anne "walked down the long hill that sloped to the Lake of Shining Waters ... Avonlea lay before her in a dreamlike afterlight ... The beauty of it all thrilled Anne's heart, and she gratefully opened the gates of her soul to it.

"'Dear old world,'" she murmured, "'you are very lovely, and I am glad to be alive in you.'"

```
S T U N T S E H C T Q R F S H Q D Q R
B E E C H W O O D R B C C E N S N W X
X E N K R D L V B Q A J N N D E C Y T
B L P Z D K Y K T R Q A Y N R R E W W
R O U L K M X S M Q O H I L L F I U M
O P F L M J R O U L X W N O H T S N Q
O E F X T L D L S C F Y Y N T M R A L
C G E C W Y P S T L O A T E N E E C I
H D D L L A A L U Y L R R B G L T D Z
W I S D E L T G Q T L I C M N A A S Z
T R L L I W X E Y M N H L O Y V W I I
M W E S M B I X R G L T V K R T G L E
H K E T K W B S M F T A X G T E N L W
J F V M Q T R O W P E V M N E L I I R
Z H E K N K D M U I X R M Y M O N G I
T R S X C D M V N G L R N P O I I Y G
T E A R O S E K R Y H S L Q E V H T H
H O N E Y S U C K L E S O X G F S R T
W N O S R E G O R S S I M N R B W A C
```

Find the words by looking horizontally, vertically, diagonally, backwards or forwards.

ARTY GILLIS	GEOMETRY	QUEENS
AVONLEA	GULF WINDS	RIDGEPOLE
BEECHWOOD	HONEYSUCKLE	SHINING WATERS
BOUGHS	LEWIS WILSON	SILAS SLOANE
BROOCH	LIZZIE WRIGHT	TEA ROSE
CARMODY	LOYALTY	TWITTERING
CHESTNUTS	MISS ROGERSON	VIOLET VALE
CROCUS	PUFFED SLEEVES	WATER FERN

Solutions

KINDRED SPIRITS page 4

ACROSS		DOWN	
1.	Prince	1.	Puffed
3.	Stacy	2.	Dress
5.	Advice	3.	Sateen
7.	Matthew	4.	Imagination
11.	Josie	6.	Ice cream
12.	Diana	8.	Hammond
13.	Currant	9.	Willow
14.	Brooch	10.	Carrots
15.	East	13.	Charlottetown
17.	Cuthbert	16.	Josephine
22.	Avonlea	18.	Boy
24.	Liniment	19.	Gilbert
26.	Plot	20.	Phillips
27.	Hope	21.	Pink
28.	Pipe	23.	Vale
29.	Sorrel	25.	Eleven
31.	Allan	30.	Red
32.	Kindred		

NAUGHTY ANNE page 5

I never do the same naughty thing twice. That's one good thing about me.

GHOSTS page 6

ACROSS		DOWN	
2.	Marilla	1.	Willow
6.	Wine	2.	Matthew
7.	Red	3.	Rachel
8.	Gable	4.	Avonlea
10.	Orchard	5.	Pasture
13.	Apples	8.	Ghosts
14.	Queen	9.	Island
15.	Slate	11.	Anne
		12.	Diana

THE WHITE WAY OF DELIGHT page 7

	A	B
1.	Cordelia	k
2.	Gilbert Blythe	f
3.	Raspberry cordial	i
4.	The Haunted Wood	h
5.	Minnie May	l
6.	Queen's	j
7.	Sorrel mare	c
8.	Mrs. Spencer	b
9.	Mrs. Hammond	e
10.	Cavendish	g
11.	Diana	a
12.	The Avenue	d

THE HAUNTED WOOD page 9

THE LILY MAID page 10

ACROSS		DOWN	
1.	Moral	2.	Auburn
3.	Marilla	4.	Abbey
5.	Jug	6.	Geometry
8.	Quilts	7.	Violetta
10.	Elaine	9.	Strawberry tart
11.	Debating	14.	Gilbert
12.	Ankle	15.	Scrumptious
13.	Matthew	16.	Peddler
15.	Scotch	17.	Beechwood
18.	Blair	19.	Amethyst
21.	Bridges	20.	Signals
22.	Avery	23.	Wincey
24.	Heart		
25.	Lock		
26.	Compositions		
27.	Dryads		
28.	Mouse		

RED HAIR page 11

Red-headed people can't wear pink, not even in imagination.

WILD CHERRY TREE page 12

ACROSS		DOWN	
1.	Birch	2.	Cherry
4.	Spring	3.	Josiah
5.	Queens	4.	Slate
6.	Romantic	7.	Carmody
10.	Frank	8.	Plum
12.	Gulls	9.	Brooch
14.	Hollow	11.	Kindred
16.	Lilac	13.	Stella
17.	Diana	15.	Bridge
18.	Puffed		
19.	Ocean		

TEACHERS page 13

	A	B
1.	Mrs. Allan	l
2.	Gilbert	i
3.	Miss Stacy	j
4.	Mr. Phillips	h
5.	Matthew	c
6.	Josie Pye	k
7.	Diana	f
8.	Mr. Allan	d
9.	Mrs. Lynde	b
10.	Anne	e
11.	Aunt Josephine	g
12.	Marilla	a

TREES AND FLOWERS page 15

ETERNAL FAREWELL page 16

ACROSS		DOWN	
2.	Chin	1.	Green
4.	Josephine	2.	Cherry
5.	Flag	3.	Matthew
6.	Ten	6.	Thomas
8.	Currant	7.	Marilla
11.	Lace shawl	8.	Croup
12.	Field	9.	Gilbert
13.	Pork	10.	Playhouse
14.	Patchwork	14.	Phillips
15.	Rachel	15.	Ridgepole
17.	Dimples	16.	Braids
21.	Exhibition	18.	Picnic
22.	Blossoms	19.	Entrance
23.	Nose	20.	Katie
24.	Seventeen		

DEPTHS OF DESPAIR page 17

This is the most tragical thing that ever happened to me.

CORDELIA page 18

ACROSS		DOWN	
2.	Cliffs	1.	Braids
4.	Pearl	2.	Cordelia
7.	Allan	3.	Sloane
8.	Vanilla	4.	Path
12.	Gossamer	5.	Laura
14.	Rose	6.	Peonies
15.	Clover	9.	Berry
16.	Violet	10.	Bubble
17.	Logs	11.	Freckles
		12.	Groves
		13.	Milton

POOR MOUSE page 19

	A		B
1.	Goods		k
2.	Aunt Josephine		f
3.	Beau		l
4.	Rosamond Montmorency		a
5.	Mr. Bentley		i
6.	Clever		h
7.	Chatter		c
8.	Jane Andrews		b
9.	Rachel		j
10.	Gilbert		e
11.	Titian		g
12.	Pudding		d

ANNE'S WORLD page 20

ANNE'S CHRISTMAS page 21

ACROSS		DOWN	
2.	Carmody	1.	Diana
6.	Spare	3.	Muriel
7.	Gilbert	4.	Rogerson
10.	Slippers	5.	Carpetbag
11.	Charlie	6.	Spencer
12.	Ribbon	8.	Josie Pye
14.	Priscilla	9.	Chocolate
17.	Laughed	12.	Rachel
19.	Beautiful	13.	Chicken
21.	Shyness	15.	Church
22.	Braid	16.	Exam
24.	Camelot	18.	Maidens
25.	Marilla	19.	Basket
		20.	Father
		21.	Sugar
		22.	Billy
		23.	Allan

GENTLE MATTHEW page 22

Well now, she's a real nice little thing, Marilla.

I'M SORRY, MRS. LYNDE page 23

ACROSS		DOWN	
2.	Katie	1.	Harmon
7.	Minnie	3.	Tresses
8.	Spare	4.	Jewel
9.	Spoil	5.	Peddler
10.	Flora	6.	Tassel
12.	Chatter	9.	Stars
15.	Apology	10.	Flag
16.	Conch	11.	Redmond
17.	Horizon	13.	Teacher
18.	Spirit	14.	Bloom

MINNIE MAY AND THE CROUP page 24

	A		B
1.	Ipecac		h
2.	Excruciatingly		f
3.	Tongue		l
4.	Geometry		k
5.	Apple		j
6.	White collar		b
7.	China		i
8.	Miss Rogerson		a
9.	Lace		g
10.	William Bell		e
11.	Buttercups		d
12.	Feather tick		c

COLORS page 25

THE AMETHYST BROOCH page 26

ACROSS		DOWN	
1.	Redmond	1.	Rachel
4.	Pincushion	2.	Mary Joe
6.	Cherry	3.	Diana
9.	Marilla	5.	Names
10.	Blewett	7.	Piano
12.	Story	8.	Matthew
13.	Honor	10.	Brook
14.	Music	11.	Tassels
18.	Pearl beads	12.	Scarecrow
20.	Ghosts	15.	Miss Stacy
21.	Top	16.	Raspberry
22.	Daring	17.	Brown
24.	Gold medal	19.	Bed
25.	Minister	23.	Green
26.	Jerry		
27.	Imagination		

DELIGHTS OF ANTICIPATION page 27

Looking forward to things is half the pleasure of them.

HORRID JOSIE PYE page 28

ACROSS		DOWN	
2.	Ankle	1.	Tart
3.	Shadow	2.	Avery
4.	Rusty	4.	Raven
6.	Ross	5.	Josie
8.	Boughs	7.	Stacy
10.	Concert	8.	Barry
12.	Poem	9.	Woodland
13.	Dory	11.	Child
14.	Fairy	12.	Pye
15.	Drunk	14.	Fun
17.	Deep	16.	Roof
18.	Farewell		

LINIMENT CAKE page 29

	A		B
1.	Aunt Josephine		c
2.	Gilbert		i
3.	Sacrifice		h
4.	Abbey Bank		k
5.	Mrs. Spencer		l
6.	Charity		a
7.	Marilla		j
8.	Butter		f
9.	Anodyne		b
10.	Rachel Lynde		g
11.	Murders		d
12.	Matthew		e

THE PICNIC page 31

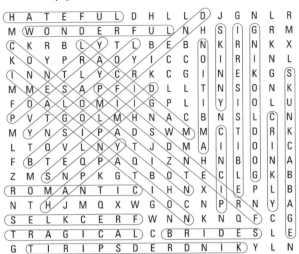

```
H A T E F U L  D H L L L  D  J G N L R
M  W O N D E R F U L  N H  S I G R M
C K R B  L Y T L  B E B  N  I R N K X
K O Y P R A O Y I C C O  I  T E S N L
I N N T L Y C R K C G  I  N  Y S O N S K
M M E S A P F I D  L L T  I  N S L D K U
F O A L O M I I G P L I  B  S O L D N
P V T G O L M H N A C M  I  N C R C N K
M Y N S I P A D S W M M  C  T D E C N K C
L T O V L N Y T J D M A  I  N B O N K A
F B T E Q P A Q I Z N H  N  C L G B B
Z M S N P K G T B O T E  X  I E P L A G
R O M A N T I C I H N X  P  R N L Y E
N T H J M Q X W G O C N  N  K N Q F C
S E L K C E R F W N N N  K N Q F C
T R A G I C A L C B R I D E S L
G T I R I P S D E R D N I K Y L N
```

BOUNCING BETS page 37

```
K Z L P I G E O N B E R R I E S C
S T F S R E W O L F K S U M L H R
E C W R B S U C O R C F A Q E D D
I L B E B M S L W H M I T S V O K
L H E K L O Z A C A S O T T O N M
I E Q R T E W P U R R H T N S W L O
L R R Y E L D I N C G U E N S F U
E R Y R P B K U C T N R R L F W N
C Y R P M T Z O H N E B C E F T
I T I P A L Z C Q T I O G G B Z R A
R F A U K W U B N L J B L I X I
Y E F G M P O N I T D E L E Y R N
X E Y J R S R E N P H L D V T R S
L T E A R O S E T Y G R W N L S H
R N L H O N E Y S U C K L E A W Q
P B L E E D I N G H E A R T M D M
```

LADY FITZGERALD page 32

ACROSS
1. Romance
4. Dream
6. Friends
7. Arthur
9. Bright River
12. Black
13. Cordelia
14. Prayers
15. Queens
19. Frills
20. Diana
22. Punishment
26. Ross
27. Spurgeon
28. Rose

DOWN
2. Chair
3. Gilbert
5. Edward
8. Wicked
10. Teachers
11. Ruby Gillis
12. Barry
16. Sewing
17. White
18. Vanity
19. Freckles
21. Sister
22. Prissy
23. Horses
24. March
25. Jane

AS GLAD AS GLAD CAN BE page 33

Do you never imagine things different from what they really are?

THE WINCEY DRESS page 34

ACROSS
3. Academy
5. Shirley
7. Spruce
10. Chimes
12. Friend
13. Sleeves
14. Moonlight
17. Emma
18. Field
19. Silver

DOWN
1. Gate
2. Wincey
4. Musk
6. Love
8. Rocker
9. Pigeon
11. Sleigh
14. Maple
15. Lynde
16. Trees

PUFFED SLEEVES page 35

	A	B
1.	Matthew	d
2.	Rosebud	l
3.	White	h
4.	Rival	a
5.	Dreams	i
6.	Waters	j
7.	Dictionary	k
8.	Puffed sleeves	c
9.	Teacher's	e
10.	Affliction	f
11.	Scope	g
12.	Garden rake	b

DIANA page 38

ACROSS
1. Roof
3. Gilbert
9. Mary
11. Titian
12. Orchard
14. Avonlea
16. Blewett
17. Puffed
19. Thomas
21. Vale
23. Cried
24. Alexander
27. Josephine
28. Manse

DOWN
1. Ruby
2. Fortunes
4. Brooch
5. Marilla
6. Matthew
7. Lawrence
8. Charlottetown
10. Mistake
13. Playhouse
14. Avenue
15. Affliction
16. Bosom
18. Children
20. Stella
22. Eyes
25. Diana
26. Raven

PRINCE EDWARD ISLAND page 39

This island is the bloomiest place. I just love it already.

THE EAST GABLE page 40

ACROSS
1. Candle
4. Wine
6. Honey
7. Sister
9. Myrtle
11. Fuchsia
14. Book
15. Muriel
16. Proverb
19. School
21. May
22. Chestnut

DOWN
2. Dryads
3. East
4. Waters
5. Shelf
8. Loyalty
10. Laura
12. Croup
13. Andrews
17. Ruby
18. Room
20. Cake

GILBERT page 41

	A	B
1.	Aunt Josephine	j
2.	Jane Andrews	k
3.	Mr. Phillips	l
4.	Miss Stacy	a
5.	Ruby Gillis	i
6.	Rachel Lynde	e
7.	Gilbert	d
8.	Mrs. Allan	h
9.	Jerry Boute	g
10.	Mrs. Barry	f
11.	Anne	b
12.	Diana	c

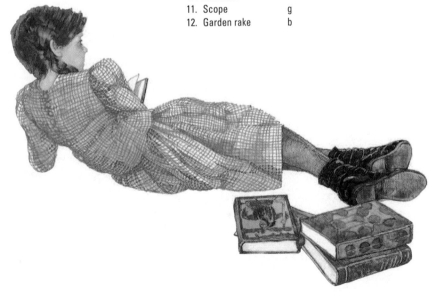

DRYAD'S BUBBLE page 43

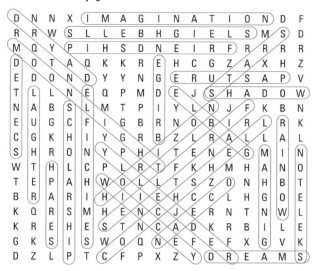

HATEFUL BOY! page 44

ACROSS		DOWN	
2.	Velvet	1.	Doctor
8.	Hair	3.	Lace
9.	Three	4.	Tennyson
10.	Blue	5.	Gilbert
12.	Sorrow	6.	Knees
14.	Humor	7.	Laughed
17.	Choir	11.	Bertha
21.	Josephine	13.	Orphan
24.	Ipecac	15.	Ministers
25.	Sleeves	16.	Shining
28.	Haunted Wood	18.	Cavendish
30.	Marilla	19.	Mustache
31.	Charlie	20.	Matthew
		22.	Plume
		23.	Beaus
		26.	Ella
		27.	Nose
		29.	Dory

DREADFUL THIN page 45

I do love to imagine I have dimples in my elbows.

THE EVENING DRESS page 46

ACROSS		DOWN	
2.	Tucks	1.	Sled
4.	Lynde	2.	Temper
6.	Diana	3.	Slate
10.	Rachel	5.	Dreams
12.	Scholarship	7.	Apple
14.	Roses	8.	Trouble
16.	Frills	9.	Braids
17.	Bridge	11.	Hopes
18.	Jerry	13.	Cherry
19.	Star	14.	Ruby
		15.	Sugar

OFF TO QUEEN'S page 47

A		B
1.	Feet	l
2.	Avery	j
3.	Slippers	g
4.	Josie Pye	a
5.	Academy	i
6.	Brooch	k
7.	Rachel Lynde	c
8.	Maid	f
9.	Katie Maurice	e
10.	Mrs. Blewett	b
11.	Wife	h
12.	Miss Stacy	d

RUBY GILLIS page 48

CURRANT WINE page 49

ACROSS		DOWN	
1.	Words	1.	Willowmere
3.	Brides	2.	Spoil
8.	Canada	4.	Stacy
9.	Cordial	5.	Spelling
11.	Sunday	6.	Marilla
13.	Minister	7.	Faint
14.	Daring	10.	Jane
16.	Hat	11.	Sweet
19.	Stumbling	12.	Diana
23.	Vanilla	14.	Drunk
24.	Aunt	15.	Ruby
25.	Imagination	17.	Christmas
26.	Grippe	18.	Unromantic
28.	Feather	19.	Skeleton
		20.	Necklaces
		21.	Knitting
		22.	Pudding
		27.	Pye

SO MANY QUESTIONS page 50

How are you going to find out about things if you don't ask questions?

SCHOOL DAYS page 51

ACROSS		DOWN	
1.	Crocus	2.	Redmond
5.	Medal	3.	Stacy
6.	Avery	4.	Teacher
7.	School	8.	Greek
9.	Ruby	10.	Maple
12.	Muriel	11.	Gilbert
13.	Phillips	12.	Music
17.	Education	14.	Latin
18.	Tart	15.	Pond
19.	Pink	16.	Boat

BIG WORDS page 52

A		B
1.	Trial	b
2.	Cry	f
3.	Ice cream	j
4.	Hopes	i
5.	Hair	l
6.	Failing	g
7.	Tomorrow	a
8.	Dream	k
9.	Loving	d
10.	Imagine	c
11.	Despair	h
12.	Delicious	e

DOCTOR SPENCER page 53

```
R W F R L W O L L O W S E D N Y L N K
K M M D E M U R I E L S T A C Y O L T
T T Y Q Y C N V C L O V E R C S O X Q
X K E N M T N E L P M I D W E V N F K
S D T Z J V E N D E N W J R C Y E R Q N F
D N A V R J Y B R D R R N P M H S N R J B T K V
N A S E J M G R I D A M G C K S N M S G K X R T S
E T I M G N D G E S U C O I R L X K T A N E F
H W J O S E P H N U Q K E L F T L N P U T C A B W R O U P
Q C H I N G I B F T P I P E I Z E T R A M H
C L K E G N I T L I U Q L H X O M K C S H N Y G
K V E H J X M M G R O V E K S P Y A S
V M
```

THE LAKE OF SHINING WATERS page 59

```
S T U N T S E H C T Q R F S H Q D Q R
B E E C H W O O D R B C C E N S N W X
X E N K R D L V B O A J N N D E C Y T
B L P Z D K Y T R Q A Y N R R E W U
R O P E F L M J R O U L X W N O H T S N Q
O G E F X T L D L S C F Y Y N T M R A
C H D D S C W Y P S T L O A T E N E C I
W I S D E L T G O T L I C M N L I Z Z I E
T R L L I W X E Y M N H L O Y A V T E W R I G H T
M W E S M B I X R G L T V K R T E L O G N I L L I
H K E T K W B S M F T A X G T E V M N I G H T
J F V M Q T R O W P E V M N E O I Y
Z H E N K D M U I X R M Y M O I V I R
T R S X C D M V N G L O N P O E G Y
T E A R O S E K R Y H S L Q E S R A
H O N E Y S U C K L E S O X G F S
W N O S R E G O R S S I M N R B W A C
```

PLAY-ACTING page 54

ACROSS
3. Bertram
5. Marilla
6. City
8. Rachel
9. Lynde
10. Sixty
14. Farewell
15. Cherry
17. Dungeons
18. Three
19. Bolingbroke
23. Phillips
24. Snow
25. Guinevere
26. Book
27. Dress
28. Teacher

DOWN
1. Lilac
2. Slate
3. Barry
4. Mayflowers
6. Club
7. Kindred
8. Resolutions
11. Work
12. Maud
13. Diana
16. Enemies
20. Gilbert
21. Apology
22. Read
23. Pigs

BOOKS page 55

I love a book that makes me cry.

A CRUSHED HEART page 56

ACROSS
3. Roof
5. Sorrel
6. Pearl
8. Tantrum
9. Candy
12. Blossom
13. Anne
14. Lane
15. Ghost
16. Cuthbert

DOWN
1. Garland
2. Nose
4. Island
5. Sixty
6. Pye
7. Prissy
10. Ipecac
11. Carrots
12. Berries
14. Love
15. Gate

FRIENDS AND FAMILIES page 57

A	B
1. Pye	j
2. Priscilla	h
3. Moody	b
4. Jerry	l
5. Chester	k
6. Cuthbert	c
7. Jane	i
8. Barry	d
9. Shirley	f
10. Rachel	a
11. Blythe	e
12. Gillis	g